This bite-sized book
a useful overview of
and help you to achi

- Establish positiv
  working
- Be productive by managing your time well
- Create an environment that supports your overall wellbeing
- Learn how to switch off and manage technology
- Put in place healthy boundaries to balance your work/home life

Success in a hybrid work environment requires employers to move beyond viewing remote or hybrid environments as a temporary or short-term strategy and to treat it as an opportunity

George Penn

What is hybrid working?

The term "hybrid working" isn't a new phenomenon because it has existed for a long time. Its prevalence however has been boosted by our experience of living through a global pandemic and having to adapt to different ways of working.

This more flexible approach enables us to spend some of our time working from home, or at another remote location, and some of our time in the workplace. This option of working can deliver some great benefits although clearly it impacts everyone differently depending on our preferences, personality, home set-up and lifestyle.

Speed, agility and
responsiveness are the
keys to future success
Anita Roddick

The future of work

We are living in the fourth industrial revolution, and this is an era that heralds huge transformation and will most certainly have a big impact on the way we live, work, and relate to one another. Technological advancement will enable us to radically look at the way we do our work and learning how to balance our lives will be fundamental to our overall wellbeing.

Being agile and responsive to new and different ways of working will help us to make the most of whatever opportunities the future has in store for us.

Successfully working from home is a skill, just like programming, designing or writing. It takes time and commitment to develop that skill

Alex Turnbull

The benefits of hybrid working

In a hybrid workplace we have an opportunity to create better life balance by integrating our work and home lives in a way that will suit us best. By avoiding some of the time-consuming commutes and choosing to work when we are feeling the most productive are just two immediate ways we can benefit.

To really make the most of the opportunity of hybrid working we will need to be more self-reliant, well organised, flexible and creative.

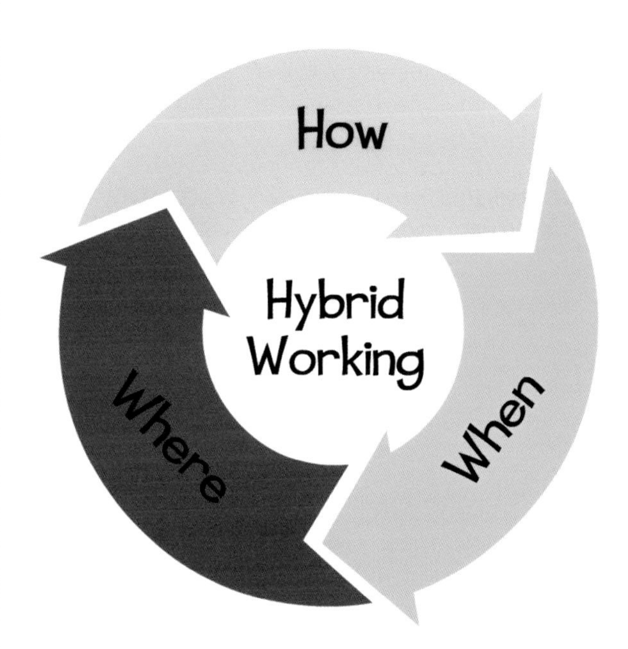
How
Hybrid
Working
When
Where

Ask questions

Asking your line manager the following questions will help you to get a clear understanding of what is required from you wherever you are working.

- What am I expected to deliver?
- What method has been agreed to monitor my workload?
- How will my performance be measured?
- How will this feed into my performance review?
- What communication is required from me?
- How and when will I communicate with you as my line manager and the team?
- What opportunity is there for collaboration?
- What resources and support are available to help me to look after my overall wellbeing?

Change might not be fast,
and it isn't always easy. But with time
and effort, almost any habit
can be reshaped
Charles Duhigg

Get into good habits

We are creatures of habit and a great deal of what we do, we do on auto pilot. It is useful to periodically check in with some of the habits we have accumulated so that we can challenge whether they are helpful and relevant.

One way to keep track of our habits is to do a self-audit by downloading an app that can help us to track everything we do, for a week. We will then be able to access a report to find out what is consuming our time. With this information, we can start to make the necessary adjustments and improvements to get into better habits.

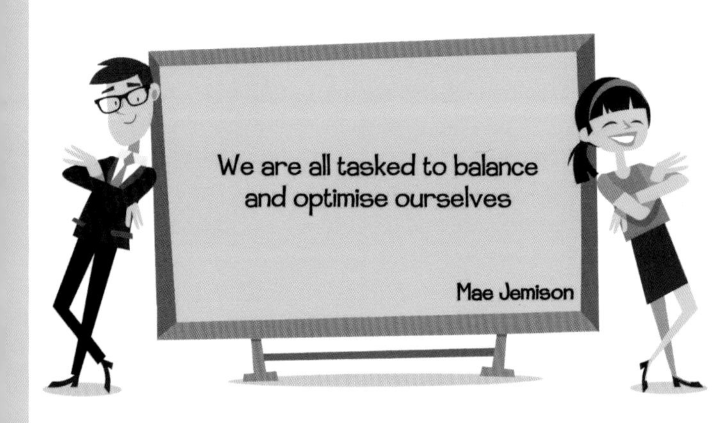
We are all tasked to balance
and optimise ourselves
Mae Jemison

How to work well anywhere

Don't work from bed.
You want your bed to be a
place of peace and calm,
not work stress
Liz Grossman

Embrace the day

Refuse the snooze and get up and get going! It is not a good idea to start our workday whilst we are still in bed.

Get up, get washed, get dressed and get going because this will help us to feel so much better about ourselves. This can also have a big impact on our energy levels, motivation and overall attitude for the rest of the day.

Top Tip – Start each day with an attitude of gratitude and boost your mood by taking some time to think about what you are grateful for in your life ☺

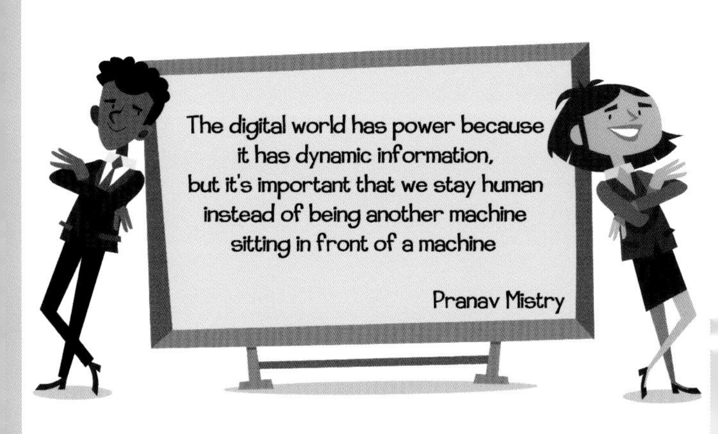
The digital world has power because
it has dynamic information,
but it's important that we stay human
instead of being another machine
sitting in front of a machine
Pranav Mistry

Take pride in your appearance

When we work from home it can be easy to fall into bad habits. Roaming about in our pyjamas or dressing gown may be the easiest option, however it won't help us feel energised.

Although it may feel like an unnecessary effort sometimes to get dressed up, it will be worthwhile. We all feel better when we smarten ourselves up and it will help us to feel more confident and professional.

Top Tip – Change your clothes at the end of the day as this is a great way to signal to your brain that your workday is over, and it is now leisure and home time ☺

Do a fake commute

One clear way to create healthy boundaries between the beginning and end of our working day is to do a fake commute to and from work.

Simply walking out of our home and around the block can help us to mentally prepare for the day ahead and it is a great way to unwind when the workday is over.

Top Tip – When you are doing your fake commute practise 'mindful' walking and be present so that you can notice what is going on in the natural world around you ☺

Define your workspace

Establishing a defined workspace, rather than roaming about, can help us to focus better and get into the right headspace to work more productively. It also helps us to put in place healthy boundaries especially when we are working from home.

It is also important to ensure that our surroundings are tidy and clutter-free because cluttered workspaces can hinder productivity by overloading our senses and making us feel stressed.

Top Tip – Build into your daily plan some time to declutter and tidy up. It can be very therapeutic and great for a quick energy boost ☺

The bad news is time flies.
The good news is you're the pilot
Michael Altshuler

Plan and structure your day

Aimlessly wandering into our day may be a lovely thing to do when we are on holiday or even on our day off; however, to get things done, planning and structuring our day is much more helpful.

Creating to-do lists for each goal and project and scheduling in proper breaks is essential for our overall wellbeing and energy levels.

Top Tip – Do the thing you least like doing first because this will make you feel lighter and more energised ☺

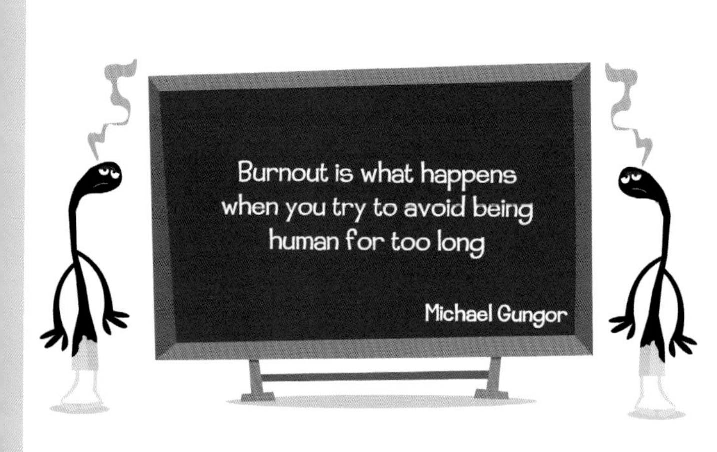
Burnout is what happens
when you try to avoid being
human for too long
Michael Gungor

Prioritise your wellbeing

When we work remotely we could find ourselves working longer hours and taking shorter breaks. As a flexible worker we may take time out for ourselves and this can trigger feelings of guilt, which then leads us to do more work. If we are not careful this can create more stress and could ultimately push us to burnout.

Hybrid working is an opportunity to work smarter not harder. This is indeed a great opportunity to shape our lives in a way that will help us to manage our stress levels and put our wellbeing at the heart of everything we do. This in turn will help us to be happier, healthier and more productive.

Top Tip – Ask your line manager what wellbeing support is available within your organisation and make the very best and most of the perks and support that is available ☺

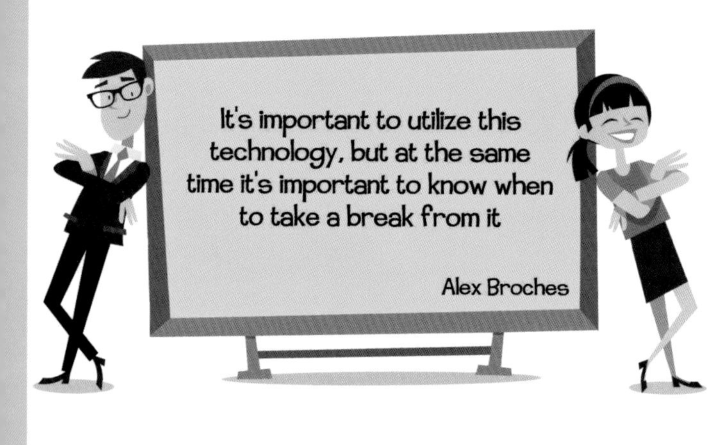
It's important to utilize this technology, but at the same time it's important to know when to take a break from it
Alex Broches

Know when to switch off

Creating moments of sanctuary in our day, and scheduling in proper breaks, is fundamental to our overall wellbeing. This is also about taking time away from technology and just being present with the world around us.

Going immediately from one meeting or task to another can be exhausting. It is far more constructive to take some time out to have rest stops, so we can clear our minds, relax and recharge.

Top Tip – Explore focused breathing exercises, mindfulness or even a bit of desk yoga which have all been scientifically proven to be highly effective for managing stress levels ☺

Enjoy proper mealtimes

To look after ourselves well and to maintain our energy levels it is important to manage the way we fuel ourselves by establishing healthy eating habits.

Skipping meals can lead to overeating on less nutritious foods due to extreme hunger which can then lead to weight gain. Planning in proper mealtimes away from our work area is far more enjoyable and much better for us.

Top Tip – For a quick healthy snack chop up your favourite fruit and vegetables and keep them in a container in the fridge or nearby to stop you reaching for unhealthy sugary alternatives ☺

Move about and stretch

An excellent mantra to adopt is “motion is the lotion”. The more we move about the more agile our bodies will be. It also stops the ‘tech neck’ pain we can get if we sit in one position for too long.

Stretching is an excellent mood-boosting activity as it releases neurochemicals in the brain, like serotonin, which is the primary chemical associated with joy and elation.

Top Tip – When you are sitting at your desk, make a point of standing up every thirty minutes to stretch and move about. Even if you only do it for a couple of minutes, it will help you feel more energised ☺

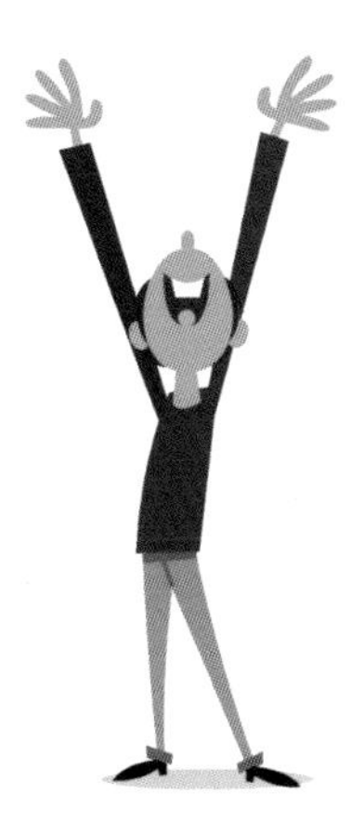

If you work from home,
especially in cold climates,
you can go days without
going outside
Michael Alexis

Get regular amounts of fresh air

Getting outside and breathing in fresh air and absorbing natural daylight is especially important wherever we find ourselves working.

Fresh air is brilliant for invigorating and stimulating the senses. So, taking breaks and getting outside as often as possible is one of the best things we can do for our overall wellbeing.

Top Tip – When you arrange a meeting with someone on a one-to-one basis why not suggest making it a walking meeting. It's a great way to exercise and increases brain function which can stimulate creativity and innovation ☺

Keep a team chatroom open.
There is nothing more important in a
group remote project than casual
communication. Not just official emails
and work updates, but the ability
to sit back and chat
David Rabin

Keep connected and communicate

Human beings are social creatures and we thrive on feeling connected to others, so building and sustaining a strong network of supportive work colleagues is essential.

Contributing to team chats and meetings is important, looking for collaboration opportunities and taking time for non-work chats are all helpful. Whenever we feel lonely or isolated it is important to reach out because we won't be the only ones who may be feeling like this.

Top Tip – Keep your team messaging apps open for quick communication and collaboration. This is just one simple way to keep connected ☺

It's not always the people who
start out the smartest who
end up the smartest
Carol S. Dweck

Love learning

The ability to learn, unlearn and relearn is essential in the dynamic and rapidly evolving world that we live in. Taking responsibility for our own development by cultivating a curious and growth mindset is the key to success.

We are all people in progress and there is an opportunity to learn something new every day.

Top Tip – Identify your own skills gaps and discuss with your line manager or work colleagues what support is available, i.e. coaching, mentoring, eLearning, training courses ☺

Celebrate success

When we anticipate achieving something, or we take time to recognise those achievements, dopamine, one of the quartet of chemicals responsible for our happiness, is released.

Relishing the opportunity to celebrate our successes, every day, no matter how big or small, will give us an instant reward boost.

Top Tip – After you have finished work write down the 3 highlights of your working day and take a few moments to sit back and reflect upon these and feel proud of what you have achieved.

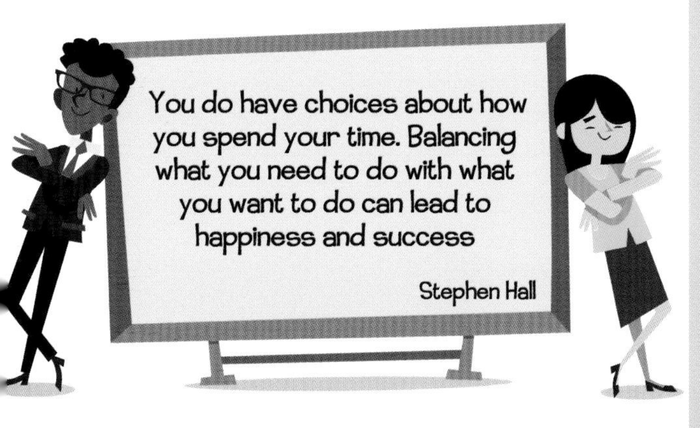
You do have choices about how you spend your time. Balancing what you need to do with what you want to do can lead to happiness and success
Stephen Hall

HYBRID WORKING

How to work well anywher

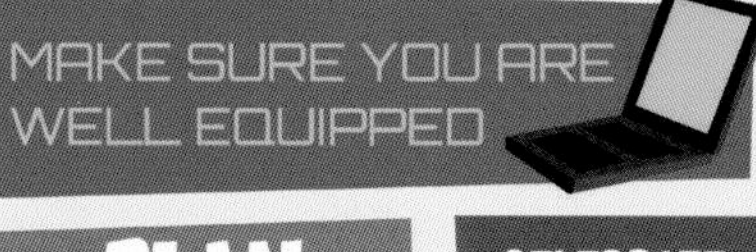

The art of life lies in the constant readjustment to our surroundings

Kakuzo Okakur

Explore more at: www.liggywebb.com

THE POCKET VÖLUSPÂ

ᚹᛟᛚᚢᛊᛈᚨ

Benjamin Thorpe Version

Edited by: Carrie Overton

Volume 1
Huginn and Muninn Publishing
ISBN: 1937571130
Library of Congress Control Number: 2014935735

For information on Asatru and Germanic Heathenry please visit our website:

huginnandmuninn.net

Hail the Aesir!
Hail the Vanir!
Hail the Folk!

VÖLUSPÂ

ᚹᛟᛚᚢᛊᛈᚨ

The Volva's Prophecy

1. For silence I pray all sacred children, great and small, sons of Heimdall they will that I Valfather's deeds recount, men's ancient saws, those that I best remember.

2. The Jötuns I remember early born, those who me of old have reared. I nine worlds remember, nine trees, the great central tree, beneath the earth.

3. There was in times of old, where Ymir dwelt, nor sand nor sea, nor gelid waves; earth existed not, nor heaven above, 'twas a chaotic chasm, and grass nowhere.

4. Before Bur's sons raised up heaven's vault, they who the noble mid-earth shaped. The sun shone from the south over the structure's rocks: then was the earth begrown with herbage green.

5. The sun from the south, the moon's companion, her right hand cast about the heavenly horses. The sun knew not where she a dwelling had, the moon knew not what power he possessed, the stars knew not where they had a station.

6. Then went the powers all to their judgment-seats, the all-holy gods, and thereon held council: to night and to the waning moon gave names; morn they named, and mid-day, afternoon and eve, whereby to reckon years.

7. The Æsir met on Ida's plain; they altar-steads and temples high constructed; their strength they proved, all things tried, furnaces established, precious things forged, formed tongs, and fabricated tools;

8. At tables played at home; joyous they were; to them was naught the want of gold, until there came Thurs-maidens three, all powerful, from Jötunheim.

9. Then went all the powers to their judgment-seats, the all-holy gods, and thereon held council, who should of the dwarfs the race create, from the sea-giant's blood and livid bones.

10. Then was Môtsognir created greatest of all the dwarfs, and Durin second; there in man's likeness they created many dwarfs from earth, as Durin said.

11. Nýi and Nidi, Nordri and Sudri, Austri and Vestri, Althiôf, Dvalin Nâr and Nâin, Niping, Dain, Bivör, Bavör, Bömbur, Nori, An and Anar, Ai, Miodvitnir,

12. Veig and Gandâlf, Vindâlf, Thrain, Thekk and Thorin, Thrôr, Vitr, and Litr, Nûr and Nýrâd, Regin and Râdsvid. Now of the dwarfs I have rightly told.

13. Fili, Kili, Fundin, Nali, Hepti, Vili, Hanar, Svior, Billing, Bruni, Bild, Bûri, Frâr, Hornbori, Fræg and Lôni, Aurvang, Iari, Eikinskialdi.

14. Time 'tis of the dwarfs in Dvalin's band, to the sons of men, to Lofar up to reckon, those who came forth from the world's rock, earth's foundation, to Iora's plains.

15. There were Draupnir, and Dôlgthrasir, Hâr, Haugspori, Hlævang, Glôi, Skirvir, Virvir, Skafid, Ai, Alf and Yngvi, Eikinskialdi,

16. Fialar and Frosti, Finn and Ginnar, Heri, Höggstari, Hliôdôlf, Moin: that above shall, while mortals live, the progeny of Lofar, accounted be.

17. Until there came three mighty and benevolent Æsir to the world from their assembly. They found on earth, nearly powerless, Ask and Embla, void of destiny.

18. Spirit they possessed not, sense they had not, blood nor motive powers, nor goodly colour. Spirit gave Odin, sense gave Hoenir, blood gave Lodur, and goodly colour.

19. I know an ash standing Yggdrasil hight, a lofty tree, laved with limpid water: thence come the dews into the dales that fall; ever stands it green over Urd's fountain.

20. Thence come maidens, much knowing, three from the hall, which under that tree stands; Urd hight the one, the second Verdandi,—on a tablet they graved—Skuld the third. Laws they established, life allotted to the sons of men; destinies pronounced.

21. Alone she sat without, when came that ancient dread Æsir's prince; and in his eye she gazed.

22. "Of what wouldst thou ask me? Why temptest thou me? Odin! I know all, where thou thine eye didst sink in the pure well of Mim." Mim drinks mead each morn from Valfather's pledge. Understand ye yet, or what?

23. The chief of hosts gave her rings and necklace, useful discourse, and a divining spirit: wide and far she saw o'er every world.

24. She the Valkyriur saw from afar coming, ready to ride to the god's people: Skuld held a shield, Skögul was second, then Gunn, Hild Göndul, and Geirskögul. Now are enumerated Herian's maidens, the Valkyriur, ready over the earth to ride.

25. She that war remembers, the first on earth, when Gullveig they with lances pierced, and in the high one's hall her burnt, thrice burnt, thrice brought her forth, oft not seldom; yet she still lives.

26. Heidi they called her, whithersoe'r she came, the well-foreseeing Vala: wolves she tamed, magic arts she knew, magic arts practised; ever was she the joy of evil people.

27. Then went the powers all to their judgment-seats, the all-holy gods, and thereon held council, whether the Æsir should avenge the crime, or all the gods receive atonement.

28. Broken was the outer wall of the Æsir's burgh. The Vanir, foreseeing conflict, tramp o'er the plains. Odin cast [his spear], and mid the people hurled it: that was the first warfare in the world.

29. Then went the powers all to their judgment-seats, the all-holy gods, and thereon held council: who had all the air with evil mingled? or to the Jötun race Od's maid had given?

30. There alone was Thor with anger swollen. He seldom sits, when of the like he hears. Oaths are not held sacred; nor words, nor swearing, nor binding compacts reciprocally made.

31. She knows that Heimdall's horn is hidden under the heaven-bright holy tree. A river she sees flow, with foamy fall, from Valfather's pledge. Understand ye yet, or what?

32. East sat the crone, in Iârnvidir, and there reared up Fenrir's progeny: of all shall be one especially the moon's devourer, in a troll's semblance.

33. He is sated with the last breath of dying men; the god's seat he with red gore defiles: swart is the sunshine then for summers after; all weather turns to storm. Understand ye yet, or what?

34. There on a height sat, striking a harp, the giantess's watch, the joyous Egdir; by him crowed, in the bird-wood, the bright red cock, which Fialar hight.

35. Crowed o'er the Æsir Gullinkambi, which wakens heroes with the sire of hosts; but another crows beneath the earth, a soot-red cock, in the halls of Hel.

36. I saw of Baldr, the blood-stained god, Odin's son, the hidden fate. There stood grown up, high on the plain, slender and passing fair, the mistletoe.

37. From that shrub was made, as to me it seemed, a deadly, noxious dart. Hödr shot it forth; but Frigg bewailed, in Fensalir, Valhall's calamity. Understand ye yet, or what?

38. Bound she saw lying, under Hveralund, a monstrous form, to Loki like. There sits Sigyn, for her consort's sake, not right glad. Understand ye yet, or what?

39. Then the Vala knew the fatal bonds were twisting, most rigid, bonds from entrails made.

40. From the east a river falls, through venom dales, with mire and clods, Slîd is its name.

41. On the north there stood, on Nida-fells, a hall of gold, for Sindri's race; and another stood in Okôlnir, the Jötuns beer-hall which Brîmir hight.

42. She saw a hall standing, far from the sun, in Nâströnd; its doors are northward turned, venom-drops fall in through its apertures: entwined is that hall with serpents' backs.

43. She there saw wading the sluggish streams bloodthirsty men and perjurers, and him who the ear beguiles of another's wife. There Nidhögg sucks the corpses of the dead; the wolf tears men. Understand ye yet, or what?

44. Further forward I see, much can I say of Ragnarök and the gods' conflict.

45. Brothers shall fight, and slay each other; cousins shall kinship violate. The earth resounds, the giantesses flee; no man will another spare.

46. Hard is it in the world, great whoredom, an axe age, a sword age, shields shall be cloven, a wind age, a wolf age, ere the world sinks.

47. Mim's sons dance, but the central tree takes fire at the resounding Giallar-horn. Loud blows Heimdall, his horn is raised; Odin speaks with Mim's head.

48. Trembles Yggdrasil's ash yet standing; groans that aged tree, and the jötun is loosed. Loud bays Garm before the Gnupa-cave, his bonds he rends asunder; and the wolf runs.

49. Hrym steers from the east, the waters rise, the mundane snake is coiled in jötun-rage. The worm beats the water, and the eagle screams: the pale of beak tears carcases; Naglfar is loosed.

50. That ship fares from the east: come will Muspell's people o'er the sea, and Loki steers. The monster's kin goes all with the wolf; with them the brother is of Byleist on their course.

51. Surt from the south comes with flickering flame; shines from his sword the Val-gods' sun. The stony hills are dashed together, the giantesses totter; men tread the path of Hel, and heaven is cloven.

52. How is it with the Æsir? How with the Alfar? All Jötunheim resounds; the Æsir are in council. The dwarfs groan before their stony doors, the sages of the rocky walls. Understand ye yet, or what?

53. Then arises Hlîn's second grief, when Odin goes with the wolf to fight, and the bright slayer of Beli with Surt. Then will Frigg's beloved fall.

54. Then comes the great victor-sire's son, Vidar, to fight with the deadly beast. He with his hands will make his sword pierce to the heart of the giant's son: then avenges he his father.

55. Then comes the mighty son of Hlôdyn: (Odin's son goes with the monster to fight); Midgârd's Veor in his rage will slay the worm. Nine feet will go Fiörgyn's son, bowed by the serpent, who feared no foe. All men will their homes forsake.

56. The sun darkens, earth in ocean sinks, fall from heaven the bright stars, fire's breath assails the all-nourishing tree, towering fire plays against heaven itself.

57. She sees arise, a second time, earth from ocean, beauteously green, waterfalls descending; the eagle flying over, which in the fell captures fish.

58. The Æsir meet on Ida's plain, and of the mighty earth-encircler speak, and there to memory call their mighty deeds, and the supreme god's ancient lore.

59. There shall again the wondrous golden tables in the grass be found, which in days of old had possessed the ruler of the gods, and Fiölnir's race.

60. Unsown shall the fields bring forth, all evil be amended; Baldr shall come; Hödr and Baldr, the heavenly gods, Hropt's glorious dwellings shall inhabit. Understand ye yet, or what?

61. Then can Hoenir choose his lot, and the two brothers' sons inhabit the spacious Vindheim. Understand ye yet, or what?

62. She a hall standing than the sun brighter, with gold bedecked, in Gimill: there shall be righteous people dwell, and for evermore happiness enjoy.

64. Then comes the mighty one to the great judgment, the powerful from above, who rules o'er all. He shall dooms pronounce, and strifes allay, holy peace establish, which shall ever be.

65. There comes the dark dragon flying from beneath the glistening serpent, from Nida-fels. On his wings bears Nidhögg, flying o'er the plain, a corpse. Now she will descend.

ᚾᛟᛏᛖᛊ

ᚾᛟᛏᛖᛋ

ᚾᛟᛏᛖᛋ

ᚾᛟᛏᛖᛋ

ᚾᛟᛏᛖᛊ

Printed in Great Britain
by Amazon.co.uk, Ltd.
Marston Gate.